JUN 0 7 1993

FEB - 6 1996

JUL 2 8 1993   FEB 2 2 1997

JAN 1 8 1994

APR 2 2 1997

MAY 1 1 1994

MAY 1 4 1997

JAN 2 8 1995   NOV 2 0 1997

MAR 1 2 1995   DEC 2 8 1998

MAY - 5 1995

MAY 2 6 1995   JAN 3 0 1999

NOV _ 6 1999

About the Book

Deep inside the cave she had dug in the snow, a mother polar bear nursed her newly born offspring during the long dark Arctic winter. As spring comes, she and her cub start to move across the tundra. The mother bear teaches him how to scout out a seal's breathing hole and kill the seal with one swipe of a paw, how to move quickly out of range of a killer whale, and how to dive underwater to catch tasty eiderdown ducks. Following the young bear from youth to maturity, Barbara A. Steiner presents an exciting picture of the mammal who is king of the Arctic. St. Tamara portrays the animals and their world with vivid realism.

Biography of a
Polar Bear

By Barbara A. Steiner

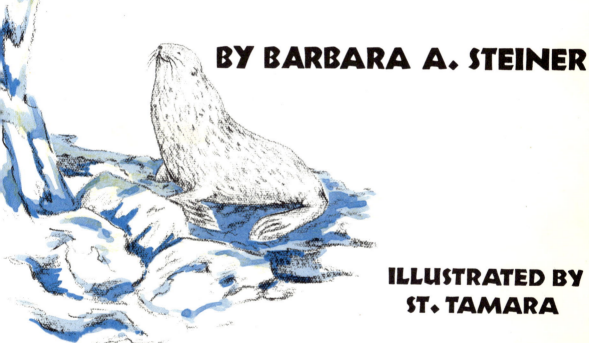

Illustrated by
St. Tamara

G. P. Putnam's Sons
New York

To my husband, Ken, for his patience and encouragement

At the top of the world in a deep snow cave a wonderful thing happened. A mother polar bear gave birth to her first baby. The tiny cub weighed two pounds and was about the size of a guinea pig. His eyes and his ears were sealed shut. His pink body was covered with a soft, thin, downy fur.

It was late December, the middle of the cold dark Arctic winter. Outside, the cub would quickly freeze. But the cave which the mother had dug was as warm as an Eskimo's snow igloo.

The cub used his sharp needlelike claws to cling to his mother and suckle her rich milk. Then he curled up in the soft fur of her hind legs and purred like a kitten. She licked his tiny face.

Through the long winter days Mother Bear dozed and nursed the cub, Nanook. He grew quickly. In six weeks his eyes and ears had opened. He crawled all around the snowy cave. By late March Nanook was three months old. He weighed about thirty-five pounds and was the size of a chubby dog. His baby hair had fallen out. Thick, soft fur had taken its place. His fur was snow white, while Mother Bear's was tinged with yellow.

Nanook was ready to follow his mother as she dug her way out of the warm snow cave. It was very cold, but a layer of fat around his body protected Nanook. His thick oily fur coat stopped the harsh, stinging winds.

He blinked his eyes several times to get used to so much light. Some bears who live in snow country suffer snow blindness, but a polar bear has sunglasses. Nanook's eyes were protected by a third eyelid coming over his eye to cut out glare.

Soon Nanook was bouncing along beside his mother, enjoying the freedom of this new white world. As far as he could see there was ice and snow.

Mother Bear raised her long neck in the cold air and sniffed. She was very hungry and stopped to eat some frozen berries sticking up through the snow. She had lived off her stored-up fat while in the snow cave.

The first three days out of the den were spent letting Nanook get used to his snowy world. While Mother Bear pawed through patches of snow for grass and berries, Nanook found a perfect sledding hill. He climbed to the top of the snow cave, then slid to the bottom. Once he was going so fast he tumbled over and over. Oof! He slammed into Mother Bear. She cuffed him playfully with her paw.

When he got tired he nursed and took a nap. At night they slept in the den.

Playing made Nanook's legs strong. But Mother Bear was hungry for the taste of seal. She decided Nanook was ready for the long walk to the pack ice. They left their snowhouse and headed north.

For a week they walked over snowy fields. Nanook grew stronger. He ran quickly after Mother Bear or followed her to the tops of icebergs. Then they slid down the other side. There were rough pads on the bottoms of Nanook's feet, and long hair grew between his toes. This kept him from slipping on the ice and helped him run in deep snow. The ice kept his long claws sharpened for climbing icebergs.

Mother Bear did not let Nanook get too tired. Often she stopped to let him suckle and sleep. But when they reached the frozen sea she was very hungry. She must find some meat quickly.

Shuffling along, she searched the ice. She came to a small iceberg and climbed to the top. Weaving her neck about like a snake, she sniffed the air. Her superb sense of smell would tell her if there was a seal within twenty miles!

Today she was lucky. Not far away she spotted a seal sleeping beside his hole in the ice. She slid down the iceberg. Then she circled so the wind was in her face. The seal would not smell her coming.

Nanook had followed. She growled, telling him to stay where he was. Nanook was glad to rest. They had walked a long way. But he was also hungry. He whimpered and patted his mother to let her know he wanted to nurse. Again she growled, warning him to be quiet.

Later Nanook would crawl along behind his mother, learning to hunt, but today he sat and watched his first lesson in stalking a seal.

Mother Bear flattened herself on the ice. Slowly she pulled herself forward. She gripped the ice with her sharp claws and pushed with her back feet.

A seal does not sleep for long. He raised his head and looked all around. Mother Bear looked like a hump of yellowish snow on the ice. The seal dozed again. Every time the seal napped the bear inched forward. The seal would see her black nose. She covered it with a white paw.

When she was close enough she galloped forward with a burst of speed. She killed the seal with one blow of her powerful paw. Then she called to Nanook.

Nanook ran to his mother. She was already eating, but she pulled off a piece of seal blubber for him. Blubber is the layer of fat which surrounds the seal's body. It is the polar bear's favorite food. Nanook sniffed at the blubber. Then he licked it with his pink tongue. It tasted different from his mother's milk, but it was good.

When Mother Bear had eaten her fill she led
Nanook back to the iceberg out of the wind.
She lay down to sleep in the spring sunshine.
Nanook drank milk until his stomach bulged.
Then he curled up to sleep beside his mother.

Crash! Screech! The wind pushed two pieces of floating ice together to make a terrible grinding noise. Mother Bear was used to such thundering noises, but Nanook woke up. He sat for a minute sticking his small black nose in the air and sniffing. Nothing else happened, so he decided to look around. Polar bears are very curious, and Nanook was no different. Since his mother was asleep he had a chance to explore.

Quickly he bounded to the top of a snowy hill. Flopping on his stomach, he sledded to the bottom. Whee! What fun! But at the bottom of the snowdrift the fun disappeared.

A huge male bear growled and blocked
Nanook's path. Nanook whimpered and backed
off. This animal looked like his mother, but
it was not friendly.

For the male polar bear Nanook was an easy meal. He may well have been Nanook's father, but this did not matter. The father bear has no part in raising babies. He was Nanook's enemy.

Nanook was no match for this thousand-pound bear. Just as the bear was about to attack, Nanook's mother hissed a warning. She leaped from the top of the hill. Placing herself between Nanook and the male bear, she growled, then roared. She was smaller than the male but would fight to the death for her cub. Backing and circling, the two bears faced each other while Nanook tried to keep out of the way.

Perhaps the male bear sensed Mother Bear's courage, or maybe he had just eaten his fill of seal blubber. He chose not to fight. Warily he backed off. Then he turned and lumbered on his way. Mother Bear nosed Nanook into place between her legs and watched the big male leave.

But the noise of the two bears quarreling had
attracted a worse enemy—man. A team of bark-
ing husky dogs raced across the ice at top speed.
An Eskimo was clinging to the runners on the
back.

Before the old male bear could escape he was surrounded by several dogs which the hunter had let loose. The bear roared and swatted at the dogs nipping at his heels. One powerful swipe sent a husky flying across the ice.

Nanook and his mother ran as soon as the danger appeared. Then a sharp crack of a rifle's bullet rang out in the cold air. Nanook looked back to see the huge bear topple onto the ice. He ran even faster after his mother's comforting shape.

Nanook would never forget the sounds and scents of the man and his dogs. They would always mean danger to him.

The next day a cold wind whipped the snow into a white fury. No seals napped in the sunshine. But Nanook's mother knew many ways to catch seals. Today she left Nanook in the shelter of a block of ice and went to sit beside a seal's breathing hole. She scraped the snow away and made the hole larger with her paw. When the seal came to breathe she would hook it out with her long claws.

The seal had many chimneys cut in the thick ice. Mother Bear had to wait until the seal came to the hole where she kept watch. She was very patient. She sat quietly, her back to the stinging wind. An hour went by.

Soon Nanook could not sit still any longer. Out onto the ice he bounded. He wanted to see if his mother would feed him. A seal can hear any sound on the ice. Mother Bear's trap was ruined. She scolded and cuffed Nanook with her large paw. He must learn to obey, or they would have nothing to eat.

Nanook's days were filled with lessons on getting food. He sat beside Mother Bear near a seal's breathing hole. He learned the scent that came from a seal's den and watched his mother jump to crash in the snow roof. The mother seal and her pups were easy prey. He would have to become a skillful hunter to survive the hard Arctic winters.

One day the ball of fire that was the sun did not go over the horizon at night. It rested on the rim of the earth, spilling out a pathway of golden light. The days grew warmer and filled with cracking sounds. The ice was melting and breaking up.

Nanook and his mother went for swims in the icy water. Floating was easy. The layers of fat around Nanook's body and the air pockets in his fur held him up. Bears' toes are partly webbed. This helps them swim fast. They paddle with their front feet and dangle their back feet in the water like a rudder.

If they went for a long swim and Nanook got tired, he grabbed hold of his mother's fur with his teeth. Sometimes he climbed on her back for a ride.

Swimming in the open water one morning, Mother Bear raised her head and sniffed the air uneasily. She stared out across the open sea. There was a churning and splashing of the water. She saw several black spikes on the surface.

Urging Nanook onto her back, she swam as fast as she could. Nearing the ice, she made long forward leaps in the water. She scrambled up onto the ice and warned Nanook to get back from the edge.

Out of the water leaped a deadly killer whale breaking the edge of the ice. Rows of sharp teeth gleamed in the sunlight. The bears ran back. Mother Bear hissed and roared.

Leaping and splashing, the killer whales moved on to other prey. They went to attack a herd of walrus swimming in the open water.

Traveling in packs, these tigers of the sea will attack anything, even a huge whale.

For several days Nanook and his mother did not go into the water. They were frightened by their narrow escape.

A polar bear can spend all his life on the ice packs and never touch land. But Nanook's mother liked the roots and berries she found there. She liked the taste of the plump eider ducks that nested on the quiet shores.

After rafting on a flat piece of floating ice, the bears swam for a time. Then they got out of the water on a large island. The earth was soft and damp. There were no trees, but many plants grew close to the ground. Flowers were blooming. Red and yellow lichen clung to rocks like painted decorations.

Nanook pushed his nose into a patch of Arctic cotton grass. He thought it was snow. It was funny to walk where there was no ice or snow.

This land is called tundra. Every summer for two months the top layer of earth thaws and plants grow and bloom hurriedly.

Mother Bear stopped to eat roots and twigs. Nanook chased an Arctic hare who had not yet changed his white coat for a brown one. A raven flew overhead scolding Nanook.

Mother Bear was headed for a long finger of water called a fjord. She knew the eider ducks swim and hatch their eggs in this fjord.

Signaling Nanook to be quiet, she entered the water backward, away from the ducks. Then she swam with only the top of her head out of water. It looked like a floating piece of ice.

The ducks dived under the water. Mother Bear dived, too. Within seconds she came back to the surface. In her mouth she held a duck. Taking it back to the shore, she shared it with Nanook.

They stayed near the fjord for several days. Nanook swam among the ducks but could not catch one. But he found a seaweed nest of greenish eggs. They were covered with a blanket of feathers. He liked the taste, so he searched for more nests.

As they wandered across the tundra a bee buzzed by Nanook's ear and landed on a patch of yellow poppies. They passed a herd of musk-oxen grazing on green grasses. Nanook watched his mother to see if she would stalk a calf that had wandered away from the herd. Nanook's mother knew the musk-oxen would gather in a circle around the baby animals. She was not hungry enough to risk a fight against those large horns.

Coming around a mound of earth, the bears found a strange sight. A brown river scampered past their feet. It was not a river of water but lemmings. There were thousands of small furry brown rodents stretched across the tundra. They were running madly over rocks, under bushes, and through puddles.

Every four or five years the lemmings' homes get overcrowded. Then they make this strange migration. Some find new homes, but many are eaten by enemies or drown in the sea.

The two bears did not question this new source of food. They flipped the lemmings aside with their paws and ate their fill.

By now Nanook was eight months old and weighed a hundred and fifty pounds. He ate everything his mother caught and a few things he found for himself. But he was still nursing. He would drink his mother's milk until he was about a year old.

Autumn was coming to the Arctic. The sun dropped below the horizon. Again there was light and dark in the Arctic day. Often northern lights shimmered and danced across the sky. The dark night was aglow with green, blue, or red.

Mother Bear and Nanook wandered on. They swam or crossed from one old ice floe to another on ice so thin a man would break right through. They traveled silently and alone. Only once did they join a crowd of other bears to feast on a whale carcass that had washed up onto the ice.

Eating and sleeping, the two bears built up a layer of fat that would help them survive the hungry winter.

Following them at a safe distance, the Arctic foxes ate the leftovers from their meals. If not for the polar bear's skill in getting food, the fox would not survive the winter.

Sometimes a snowy owl flew down for some scraps.

Once the bears tried to stalk a young walrus that was away from the herd. The youngster squealed, and the walrus herd came to the rescue. The two bears ran. There was easier food to catch. A two-thousand-pound walrus with razor-sharp tusks can kill a big bear.

In December the sun no longer came over the horizon. The winter darkness had come. The stars helped to light the land, however. On moonlit nights the icebergs cast eerie shadows over the sparkling blanket of snow.

Except for females who are having babies, polar bears do not hibernate. Sometimes Nanook and his mother slept through the fierce Arctic storms. Then they would wake and search again for food.

Often they were hungry, but the two bears worked together to catch seals. When they found a series of breathing holes, Mother Bear would sit at one. Nanook jumped to break the ice around the other holes. The seal knew Nanook could catch him at the larger holes, so he was forced to breathe at the hole where Mother Bear waited.

By late winter the bears were thin and hungry all the time. Then one day at noon in early February, Nanook blinked his eyes. The sun was peeking over the horizon. The long winter darkness was over.

Spring was coming. The days would grow longer. Seals would come out on the ice to greet the sunny days. Food would become easier to catch.

Nanook slid down a snow hummock and ran playfully beside Mother Bear. He was half as large as she but would be under her care for another year. There was still much to learn about living in this cold, hard land.

She would teach him more tricks about catching food and where to find it. He would learn the pathways of their Arctic home.

In another spring she would leave to have more cubs, usually twins. Then Nanook would take his place as king mammal of the Arctic world.

About the Author

Barbara A. Steiner has been a third-grade teacher, a reading specialist, and a librarian. She has written extensively for magazines and is a member of the National Writer's Club, National Wildlife Association, and the Audubon Society. Mrs. Steiner lives in Boulder, Colorado, with her husband and two daughters.

About the Artist

St. Tamara was born in Byelorussia. She studied art in the United States at the Art Students' League and at Columbia University, where she received a Master's of Fine Arts. She is a free-lance artist and designer and lives with her husband in Ocean, New Jersey.